Curriculum Foundation Series

ART STORIES
BOOK THREE

BY
WILLIAM G. WHITFORD
EDNA B. LIEK AND
WILLIAM S. GRAY

Life—Reading Service

SCOTT, FORESMAN AND COMPANY
CHICAGO · ATLANTA · DALLAS · NEW YORK

Grateful acknowledgment is made to the author
and to the publishers for permission to reprint "The
Artist," by Anna Bird Stewart, from *The Gentlest
Giant*, published by Robert M. McBride and
Company.

377.4

PREFACE

Art Stories, Book Three is the third of a group of books on the appreciation of art. This group and similar ones in other subjects make up the Curriculum Foundation Series. Each group of books provides reading and study experiences in a specific field which parallel and reënforce oral learning-activities.

Art Stories, Book Three provides opportunity to inculcate in the child an appreciation of beauty. It develops further the teaching of *Art Stories, Books One* and *Two* and introduces additional simple but significant art concepts.

Through varied pictures and interesting reading the child is made increasingly conscious of beauty of color, form, and line as seen in nature, in pictures, in all his surroundings. Elementary ideas of drawing, painting, sculpture, design, architecture, interior decoration, costume, and civic art are thus introduced in a setting of natural child interests and activities.

The reading and discussion of such a book will enable pupils to see new beauty in the familiar things of life and will arouse in them an interest in many forms of art.

Art Stories, Book Three has been painstakingly edited with regard to reading difficulties—especially in sentence structure and the introduction and repetition of words. The vocabulary is correlated with that of *Art Stories, Books One* and *Two* and is so carefully controlled that this book may be read without difficulty by any average third-grade group.

STORIES

PART THREE—LANDSCAPES

PART FOUR—ARCHITECTURE

PART FIVE—DESIGN

PICTURES

Several of the works of art listed below are here reproduced from the originals for the first time. Others are reproductions of paintings, etchings, photographs, or illustrative work that has previously been published. To the owners of these works or of the copyrights we are deeply grateful.

The remaining pictures are by the following well-known illustrators: Helen Hudson Below, L. Kate Deal, Gordon Ertz, Lawrence Guetthoff, Miriam Story Hurford, Gertrude Kay, Alexander Key, Electra Papadopoulos, Herbert N. Rudeen, Keith Ward, Mariel Wilhoite. The cover design was made by Mr. Key, and the end sheets were designed by Mr. Rudeen.

Part One
COLORS

Nancy and the Artist

In the summer Nancy was visiting her cousins. One day the children went to the woods and had a picnic.

After lunch Peter said, "Let's play a game. We can hide among the trees."

"All right," said Barbara. "I'll be it."

Away ran the children. Nancy went straight into the woods, and soon she came to a path.

"I'll go along this path until I come to a big tree," she thought. "Then I'll hide behind it."

She went on and on. Now and then she saw a big tree, but each time she thought, "I can find a bigger one."

Suddenly she came to the edge of the woods.

9

There she saw a woman. In front of the woman was a picture on a stand.

"Hello," said Nancy. "May I see what you are doing?"

"Yes," said the woman. "I am painting a picture of the woods."

"Oh, you are an artist!" cried Nancy. "But I never saw a picture standing on legs before."

The artist laughed. "This is an easel," she said. "It holds the picture while I am painting."

Nancy stood by the artist and watched her paint. The little girl looked at the woods, and then she looked at the picture.

After a while she said, "All the trees in the woods are green, but they are not all the same green. In your picture I see different kinds of green."

"Look at that tall tree near the path," said the artist. "Its leaves are yellow-green. I am going to paint that tree in my picture."

"Can you paint it with that green paint you have?" asked Nancy.

"No," answered the artist. "I'll have to put some yellow in this green."

Nancy watched the artist as she mixed the yellow-green color and painted the tree.

The artist asked, "Do you see why this color is called yellow-green? It is between yellow and green. We might call yellow-green an in-between color."

Nancy asked, "Are there any other in-between colors?"

"Yes," said the artist. "There are five others. One of them is between blue and green. What do you think that color is called?"

"Is it blue-green?" asked the little girl.

"Yes, it is," said the artist. "Here is some blue-green. It has both blue and green in it. See how different it is from yellow-green.

"There are six in-between colors. Each one is made by mixing two rainbow colors. See if you can think of the other in-between colors."

First Nancy said, "The rainbow colors are red, orange, yellow, green, blue, and violet.

"Red and orange make red-orange. Yellow and orange make yellow-orange. Those are two of the in-between colors.

"You showed me yellow-green and blue-green. Let me see! The next in-between color must be blue-violet."

"And the last one is red-violet," said the artist.

Just then Nancy's cousins came running out of the woods.

"Why, Nancy!" Peter cried. "How well you hid! We looked and looked, but we couldn't find you anywhere."

Nancy laughed. "I never hid at all," she said. "I forgot about hiding.

"This artist told me about in-between colors. It was so interesting that I didn't remember you were looking for me."

12

In-between Colors

This is a picture of the artist and the children.

Nancy is wearing a blue-violet dress. Where is she standing?

Peter has a red-violet sweater. Tell which boy is Peter.

Barbara's dress is red-orange. Which girl is Barbara?

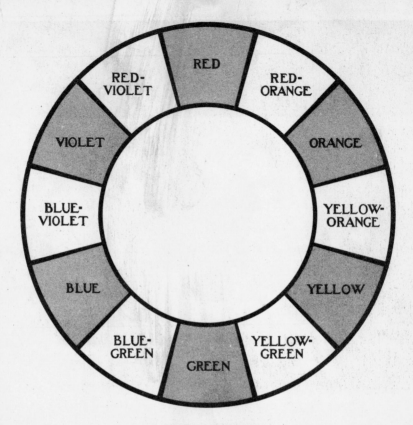

A Color Wheel

This page shows a wheel with the names of colors on it. Find the names of the six rainbow colors.

The other colors named on the wheel are the ones that Nancy and the artist called in-between colors. Why did they think this was a good name for these colors?

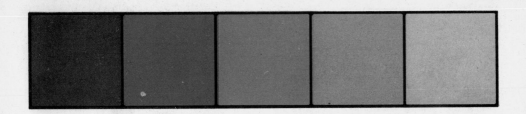

Tints and Shades

You can make any color lighter by mixing white with it. The more white you put in, the lighter the color becomes. Light colors are called tints.

Mixing black with a color makes it darker. The more black you put in, the darker the color becomes. Dark colors are called shades.

You can make a tint or a shade of any rainbow color or of any in-between color.

Look at the colors at the top of this page. Which are the light reds? Light red colors are called tints of red. Which are the dark reds? Dark red colors are called shades of red.

Look at the colors below. Find tints of green. Find shades of green.

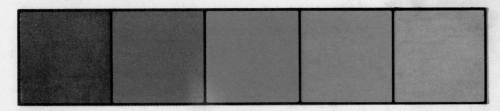

How the Cottage Was Named

One day in the fall Paul and Nancy went to the woods. They were with Mr. Banks and his wife, who had a new cottage.

The cottage stood on a high hill. Around it were many trees that had bright autumn leaves.

"How pretty the trees look from this hill!" cried Paul, as he stood in front of the cottage. "Look at all the different colors."

"I can see some in-between colors," said Nancy.

"There are red-violet and red-orange leaves, and far away I see some yellow-orange."

"Paul, what in-between colors can you see?" asked Mrs. Banks.

The boy answered, "I see yellow-green leaves, and some of the trees look almost blue-green."

"I can see tints and shades of autumn colors," said Nancy, as she broke off a small branch that had colored leaves. "Here are light red and dark red, and this leaf is dark red-orange."

"The colors in the sunlight are brighter than those in the shadow," said Paul.

Just then the sun hid behind a cloud.

"Let's go into the house," said Mr. Banks.

As they went up to the cottage, Paul asked, "What is the name of your cottage?"

"It has no name," answered Mr. Banks. "Perhaps you and Nancy can think of a good name."

"We'll try," said the children.

When they were in the cottage, Mrs. Banks asked, "Would you like to look at our pictures? We have many pictures which show outdoor colors at different seasons of the year."

"Oh, yes!" cried Nancy, going up to a picture that was hanging on the wall. "Here is one with bright fall colors like those we've seen today."

Walter Koeniger.

"Here is a picture of a winter scene with many
bright colors," said Paul. "It is just as bright as
the autumn picture, Nancy."

Mrs. Banks said, "This is the picture I like best of all. Notice the colors the artist put in it. See the golden tints on the snow. There are spots of yellow-orange on the trunks and branches of the trees, too."

"The evergreen trees are a very pretty color," said Nancy. "And there are blue, green, and violet colors in the water."

"Look, Paul!" cried Mr. Banks. "The sun has just come out again. Sunlight makes colors beautiful in pictures and out of doors."

Paul looked at the lovely colors in the sunshine. Then he said to himself in a soft voice, "I have thought of something!"

He ran out of doors, but in a minute he was back. "I wanted to see your cottage with the sun shining on it," he said, as he shut the door. "I have thought of a good name.

"Let's call it Sunshine Cottage, because it has sunshine colors all around it and sunshine colors in the pictures inside."

"Oh, yes!" cried Nancy. "Even when it's dark and cloudy outdoors, you can enjoy the sunlight colors in your pictures."

"That is a good name," said Mrs. Banks. "We will call it Sunshine Cottage."

A Picture of Jack Frost

You have often heard made-up stories about fairies. One kind of fairy is an elf.

In this picture the artist tells a story about an elf. The name of the elf is Jack Frost. Doesn't he look queer? The artist made him so small that he can sit on the stem of a leaf.

The elf is painting the leaves in the fall. Every leaf Jack Frost paints is different. Notice the beautiful autumn colors.

The leaf he is working on has different colors. Name them.

Where do you see some dark leaves? What colors do you see in the other leaves?

There are many different colors in the background. Some are dark, and some are light. Name some of the colors in the background.

Jack Frost's clothes are a light blue tint. The light blue stands out against the darker background of the picture.

The artist has made the leaves large, and placed them so that they look well in the picture.

The man who drew and colored this picture of Jack Frost is an artist who has made many pictures.

John T. McCutcheon.

Golden Hour

Golden in the garden,
  Golden in the glen;
Golden, golden, golden
  September's here again!
Golden in the tree-tops,
  Golden in the sky;
Golden, golden, golden
  September's going by.*

In autumn the woods are dressed in golden colors. We see yellow, yellow-green, orange, and red-orange.

On the next page there is an autumn picture that shows golden colors. It was painted by an artist named Metcalf. He called it "Golden Hour," because it shows the time of day when outdoor colors look brightest.

The sunlight makes the leaves and grass look bright. In the foreground there is a tall tree which is yellow-orange. The next tree is green and yellow-green.

Look at the colors in the shadows. They are darker than those in the sunlight.

There are many beautiful in-between colors in this picture. Name the ones you see.

*Reprinted by permission from *For Days and Days* by Annette Wynne. Copyright 1919 by Frederick A. Stokes Company.

Willard Metcalf.

Mr. Metcalf loved outdoor colors and painted
many outdoor pictures.

23

Pictures in Black, White, and Gray

Every Friday Miss Bush came to the Ray School to help the children with their art work.

One day she said to the class, "Today we will make pictures without using colors. You are to use only black, white, and gray paint. Do you remember how to make gray?"

"I know!" cried Ann quickly. "You mix black and white to make gray."

"That is right," answered Miss Bush.

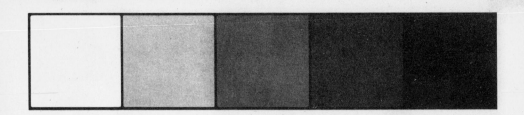

"But there are different kinds of gray. The more white you put into gray, the lighter it gets. The more black you put in, the darker it gets."

She held up a chart. "How many kinds of gray do you see on this chart?" she asked.

"I see three kinds of gray," answered Billy.

Miss Bush said, "The gray next to the black is dark gray. The one nearest white is light gray. The gray in the middle is called middle gray."

"Why, these grays are like steps that go from black to white!" cried Jack.

"Yes, they are," said Miss Bush. "Now you may make your pictures. Use black, white, and the different kinds of gray that you know."

Helen said, "My paper is white. Shall I put white paint on it?"

"No," answered Miss Bush. "Where you want white in your picture, you may let some of the paper show. But if you had colored paper, you would have to use white paint instead."

All the children made black, white, and gray
pictures. Bobby painted a big gray engine, but
Miss Bush liked Mary's picture of an elephant
best of all. It is not too dark and not too light.

The different kinds of gray look well together.
They look well with the black and white, too.

Find dark gray in this picture. Find light gray.
Where do you see some middle gray?

We often see pictures that are made with black,
white, and different kinds of gray. Point out the
different kinds of gray in some pictures.

Do You Know Colors?

If you have a box of paints with the six rainbow colors in it, you can make other colors by mixing.

What color will you get if you mix red and orange paints?

If you put yellow and green together, what color will you get?

What color will blue and violet make?

Name some other in-between colors that you can make by mixing two of the colors in your paint box.

If you have a pan of black and a pan of white paint, you can make shades and tints of all the colors in your paint box. You can make shades and tints of the in-between colors, also.

How would you make a tint of red?

How would you make a shade of red?

How would you make gray?

Ask someone to show you pictures by well-known artists, such as Mr. Metcalf.

Notice the different colors which these artists used in their paintings.

When you go for a walk, look about you and find as many different colors as you can.

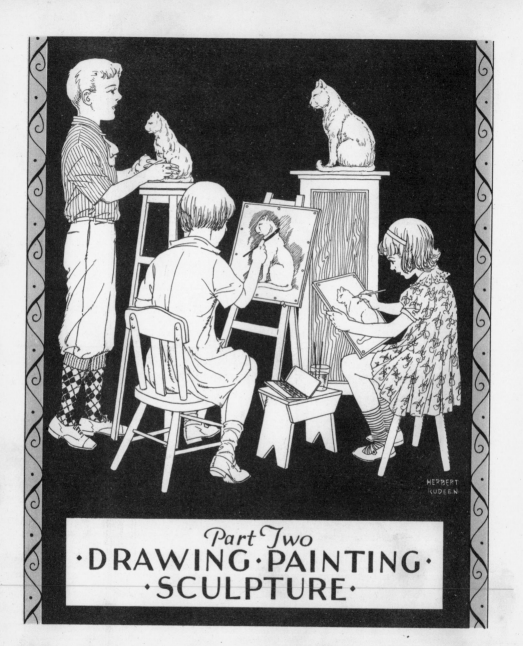

Part Two
· DRAWING · PAINTING ·
· SCULPTURE ·

HERBERT RUDEEN

The Farm Babies

Alice's big brother Tom went to an art school in the city.

Tom usually came home to the farm on Friday evening, and then Alice was happy. She loved to look at the drawings he had made at school.

One Friday when Tom came home, his sister was watching for him.

"Tom," she cried, "we have a surprise for you! It is out in the pasture. Come quickly and see what it is."

Tom took his sister's hand, and they ran to the pasture as fast as they could.

They stood at the fence and looked around.

Just then a horse and a colt came running up to the fence.

"See!" cried Alice. "Molly has a little colt."

Tom laughed at the way the colt ran and played beside its mother.

"What long, thin legs the colt has!" said Tom. "I will draw a picture of him."

He took out a small drawing book and a lead pencil and began to make a line drawing.

As he worked, he said to Alice, "Drawing quickly like this is called sketching.

"Artists nearly always make sketches of the things they want to put into their pictures. They make sketches so that they will remember how the things looked."

In a short time Tom had made three or four sketches of the colt. His sister was very much pleased with them.

"Do you think you could show me how to sketch, Tom?" she asked.

"Why, yes," answered Tom, as they turned away from the pasture. "We'll go right now and make some sketches of other baby animals on the farm."

So Alice and her big brother went to see the little pigs.

Tom said, "When you draw an animal, you must notice its shape. A baby pig has a curved

back. There are curves in its legs and head, also. Even its ears have short curves."

After Tom had made a sketch of a baby pig, Alice made one, too. Then Tom drew a puppy that was playing in the yard.

Alice said, "Please make some more sketches. I'd like pictures of all the baby animals on our farm."

So he drew pictures of all the farm babies.

Here are some of the sketches that Tom made
for his little sister with his lead pencil. See how
well he drew these animals with just a few lines.
Point out lines that curve.

The Sketching Class

One Saturday afternoon Helen and Bobby
went to a sketching class. The artist, Miss King,
came to meet them at the door.

As they walked into the big workroom, Miss
King said, "This room is called the studio. A
studio is a room where an artist does painting,
drawing, or modeling."

The studio was full of children working at easels.

There was a big box in the middle of the room.
It was upside down, and a boy was standing on it.

"Why is John standing on the box?" asked
Bobby.

"John is posing," answered Miss King.

"He stands very still while the other children draw pictures of him. When he gets tired, one of the other children will take his place."

"I'd like to pose," said Bobby. "I think it must be easier to pose for a picture than to make one."

Miss King laughed. "Very well, Bobby," she said. "You have a nice sailor suit. I know the children would like to draw a sailor boy."

So Bobby stood on the box and posed.

The artist gave Helen an easel, a drawing-board, some paper, and some crayons. Then the little girl began to draw a picture of Bobby. The artist helped her.

As they worked together, Miss King said, "Drawings of people are called figure drawings. We will make a figure drawing which shows the shape of Bobby's head and the shape of his body in his sailor suit.

"Sometimes figure drawings are made in black, white, and gray. Sometimes they are colored. You may color your drawing if you wish."

So Helen colored her drawing, and Miss King helped her make a border around it.

When the children had finished their pictures of Bobby, the artist asked Helen to pose.

She said, "You may be a cook. Put on this cap
and apron."

Each child made a figure drawing of Helen in
her cap and apron.

Bobby and Helen hid their pictures until Mother's
birthday. Then the two children gave her the
figure drawings they had made in the artist's
studio.

Mother liked the two drawings better than
anything the children had ever given her. She
called one "The Sailor Boy," and the other, "The
Little Cook."

Animals As Artists Show Them

Some artists paint colored pictures. Some artists make statues. And some artists draw with a lead pencil, a pen, or crayons.

On the next page there is an artist's drawing of some colts. Pictures of this kind are made with just a few lines.

The artist who drew this picture made the colts large enough to look well in the space.

She must have enjoyed watching the two colts galloping around on their long, thin legs. She has shown us how funny they looked to her.

The colts seem surprised to see each other. Each one looks as if it were saying, "Well, who are you?"

There are only a few lines in this picture. But there are enough to show how full of play the colts are. They seem ready at any minute to jump and gallop away.

The artist has shown the shape of the colts' bodies and their long, thin legs. Some of the lines are curved, and some are almost straight. Some lines are dark, or heavy, while others are light.

There are heavy lines in the heads, the manes, and the tails of the colts.

Courtesy Chicago Book & Art Auctions, Inc.

Renée Sintenis.

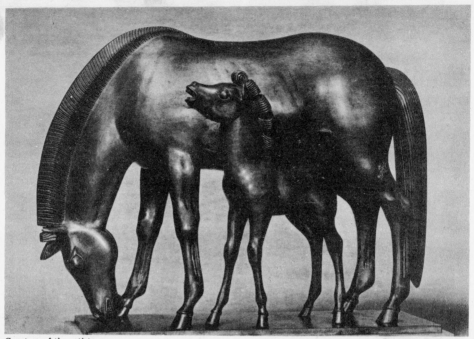

Lawrence T. Stevens.

Here is a statue of a colt standing beside its mother. A sculptor made this statue. It is not flat, like a drawing. It is rounded and made of metal.

In the picture you can see only one side of the statue. But if you could see the statue itself, you could walk around it and look at it from the front, back, and sides.

Don't you wish you could see this statue from all sides?

A sculptor has to know how animals look from all sides. In his statues he shows how round their bodies are.

The horse's body is beautiful. Her back and sides are rounded, and her legs are well-shaped.

The colt's body has many curves. It is beautiful, and the long, thin legs make lovely lines.

The artist has shown the lines and forms of the little colt and its mother.

He has not made them look just like real animals. Look at the colt's mane. It is modeled with curving lines that curl over the neck.

In the picture on page 37, how did the artist show the colts' manes?

The horse's neck is long and curved. Her back and tail are modeled with curving lines, too. The hair of her mane and tail is shown by many lines. The artist made the lines over and over again, like a design.

If there are any statues in your school, look at them from all sides. See how the artist has modeled their forms.

Look again at the line drawing of the colts on page 37. In what way is a statue different from a line drawing?

A statue is different from a painting, too.

39

Othmar Hoffler.

Here is a painting that shows a horse and a colt. The artist called this picture "Barnyard Animals."

The horse and the colt are in the foreground of the picture.

An old barn is shown in the background.

Look at the side of the barn. The lettering and pictures make spots of color on the wall.

The shape of the barn stands out clearly against the light sky behind it.

There are lovely tints in the sky. Name the colors that you see in it.

Name some other colors that you see in the picture.

There are many straight lines and many curved lines in this picture. Point out a few of the curved lines.

Most paintings have colors, but line drawings and statues are not usually colored.

A painting has a background, too, while a statue does not have a background. Usually a line drawing does not have a background.

Now you have seen a drawing, a painting, and a statue of horses.

Look again at the drawing on page 37, the statue on page 38, and the painting on page 40.

In what way are the drawing, the painting, and the statue all alike?

In what ways are they different?

The Artist's Daughter

Once there was an artist who painted a picture of his daughter. Maybe she came to his studio and posed for him, while he painted the picture shown on the next page.

The most important thing in this picture is the figure of the little girl. So we call this a figure painting.

Notice how well the figure fills the space of the picture. It is just large enough.

The artist has shown how the girl looked in her long, light-colored dress. The dark background makes the child's figure in the light dress stand out clearly.

She has brown eyes. Her dark hair looks pretty with her round, rosy face.

The colors in the picture look well together. We see brown and red. Name some different kinds of red that you see in the picture.

What other colors do you find? Where do you see these colors?

This beautiful figure painting is called "The Artist's Daughter."

Find another figure painting in your art book and tell what page it is on.

Friedrich A. von Kaulbach.

43

A Statue of Red Riding Hood

Here is a statue which shows Little Red Riding Hood. The wolf is standing just behind her.

The child seems to be saying something to the wolf. Perhaps she is telling him that she is going to see her grandmother.

This statue was carved out of stone.

First the sculptor designed the statue. When an artist plans how something is to be made, we say he designs it.

The sculptor designed the rounded forms of the little girl and the wolf by modeling them in the soft clay. Then he cut the figures out of a large stone block. The stone figures looked just like the figures he had modeled.

Notice the lines which are carved in Little Red Riding Hood's dress and the carved lines on her basket.

Carved lines show the little girl's hair near the edge of her cap. There are lines in the hair on the wolf's neck, also.

This lovely statue is in a park in a country far away. Children often play around it. They like to look at it and remember the story of Red Riding Hood and the wolf.

Ignatius Taschner.

45

The Artist

Pencils have a million pictures
Shut way up inside their lead;
All you have to do is draw them,
Or have Uncle draw instead.

There are steam and sailing vessels,
Engine trains with curling smoke,
Homes with sidewalks and with fences,
And—oh, my, *the pencil broke.*

Three Kinds of Art

In this part of your art book you have learned about three kinds of art—drawing, painting, and making statues.

Drawings are made with a lead pencil, a pen, or crayons. Different kinds of lines are used in drawings. They may have curved lines or straight lines.

Look at the drawing on page 37. It shows nothing but the colts. Only a few lines are used. But they show us how full of play the colts are.

A painting usually shows us things in color. The painter chooses colors that look well together. He arranges the things to make a beautiful picture.

The artist who models or carves is a sculptor. A sculptor shows the important lines in the things he models. He makes lovely statues by modeling or carving beautiful forms.

Look again at the picture which shows the statue of the horse and colt. In the statue we see the beautiful lines and forms of the animals' bodies.

In what way is a line drawing different from a painting?

How is a painting different from a statue?

Part Three
LANDSCAPES

The Artist's Joke

Joe and Betty were visiting their uncle at his summer home. Uncle Dick was an artist, and the children loved to watch him paint.

Uncle Dick said that his paintings showed outdoor scenes and so they were called landscapes.

One Saturday Joe and Betty went with their uncle to watch him paint. He put up his easel and began to paint a landscape.

Betty and Joe sat and watched him.

Suddenly Betty turned to Joe.

"Look," she said, as she pointed to her uncle's drawing. "Uncle Dick forgot something. See that big red barn. He hasn't put that in his picture. He has painted the trees and the hills just as if the barn were not there."

"Yes, he did forget the barn!" Joe cried. "Let's play a joke on him. I'll get my camera and take a picture of this same scene. My picture will show the barn, because a camera sees everything just as it is."

"Oh, do!" said Betty. "Uncle Dick will be surprised when he sees our picture and finds that he forgot to put the barn in his painting."

The children walked away.

In a few minutes they came back with Joe's camera and took a picture of the scene. Then they ran off, laughing as they went.

The next day their picture was finished, and Joe and Betty took it to their uncle. He was looking at the landscape he had painted.

"We know a good joke on you, Uncle Dick," said Betty.

"What is it?" asked Uncle Dick, smiling at the children. "What have I done now?"

Joe answered, "You forgot to put the barn in your painting. So we took a picture with my camera to show you how the scene really looks."

50

Uncle Dick laughed and said, "I did not forget the barn. I think my picture looks better without it.

"A camera puts everything it sees in a picture, but an artist can choose the things that look best in his picture."

The children looked at their uncle's painting and then at the picture they had taken.

They were surprised to see how different the two pictures were.

Joe said, "I see that you have left out other things besides the barn."

"And you have put in some things that are not in the picture we took," said Betty. "Look at those clouds! Our picture does not show any clouds."

Uncle Dick said, "When you take a picture with a camera, you show things just as they are.

"Your camera cannot plan a picture, as an artist does. I design a picture before I paint it. That means I plan it. I try to paint only the things that will make my picture beautiful.

"In this picture I did not want to show any buildings. So I did not put in the barn. But I painted clouds with beautiful shapes and colors."

While the children were looking at the two pictures, Uncle Dick told them more about how artists design their pictures.

He said, "First of all, an artist decides what he wants in the foreground.

"Then he plans the background and other parts of the picture. He arranges the different parts so that they will look well together. Everything is planned to make the picture beautiful."

M.S. HURFORD

For a long time Joe and Betty looked at Uncle Dick's painting on the easel and at the picture they had taken with the camera.

At last Joe said, "Uncle Dick, I didn't know that artists plan their paintings so carefully. I think the picture you painted is much prettier than our picture."

Betty laughed and said, "When we took the picture, we thought we had a joke on you. But the joke was on us, instead."

A Famous Landscape

On the next page there is a print of a landscape by an artist named Corot.

Corot was a great landscape painter. He made many lovely pictures of country scenes, and he made some pictures of people, too.

The picture on the next page shows a beautiful scene with trees and grass and sky.

It shows early morning, a time of day that Corot liked to paint. The sun is just coming up. How beautiful the out-of-doors looks in the early morning light!

Corot liked to paint the lines and forms of trees. In this picture he shows the lovely curves of the trees.

The branches and leaves seem to be moving softly in the morning wind. We cannot see the different leaves, but we see their green color.

There are many kinds of green in the grass, too.

In the picture there are some dancers. Their clothes make bright spots of color that look well with the greens and browns of the out-of-doors. What colors do you see in their clothes?

Name some other colors that you see in the picture.

Camille Corot.

This is a famous picture. People have admired it for many years. It was painted a long time ago, but it has never been forgotten.

Corot painted other famous pictures, too. Many people own prints of them. Perhaps there are some prints of Corot's pictures in your home or school. Look for copies of his landscapes and notice the beautiful way he painted outdoor scenes.

55

Light and Dark in Pictures

You have looked at the colors and the curved lines in the landscape that Corot painted.

Corot arranged the light and dark parts of this picture in a beautiful way.

The drawing on this page shows how he arranged them. Corot's picture is lovely, even when we do not see its colors.

The sunlight and shadow make beautiful light and dark spaces in the picture. That is one reason why people admire it.

Notice that the dark spaces are not all in one part of the picture. There are dark spaces at each side. Some dark places are above, and some are below.

The dark forms of the trees show clearly against the light sky. Notice the large trees at the right of the picture. They have light around them.

The light goes up around the large trees and comes over their tops and down into the middle of the picture. What a lovely curve of light this is! There is light around the trees at the left, too. The sunshine makes light places among the dark shadows on the grass. There are dancers both in sunshine and in shadow.

Many colored paintings have interesting light and dark spaces. Find some prints of landscapes and look for light and dark in them.

Hold a thin piece of paper over one of the pictures. By drawing carefully on this paper try to show the light and dark parts of the picture.

Your drawing will show how the artist arranged the lights and darks in the picture.

Jane Learns to Draw

Jane was not so old as John and Polly, and had not gone to school so long as they had. But she loved to play with the other children, and she tried to do the things they did.

One day she was playing school with Polly and John. Polly was the teacher.

"This is the art class," said Polly. "You may each draw a landscape. You may put a house and some trees in it."

Jane took her crayons and began to draw.

But John did not start drawing at once. He
had learned to plan a picture before he drew it.

He decided how large to make the trees and
the other things, so that they would fill the space.

When the children had finished, Polly put their
drawings side by side on a piece of cardboard.

Polly looked at Jane's drawing and said, "The
house and the trees in this picture are too small.
They do not look well, because there is too much
space left around them.

"But don't look so unhappy, Jane. I will show
you how to make a better picture."

Then Polly looked at John's drawing. He had
made a house with some large trees around it.

The house was not too small, and the trees reached
the top of the picture.

Polly said, "This is a good picture, John."

Henri Lerolle.

Then Polly was ready to help Jane.

"Now, Jane, I will help you make a better picture," she said.

But Jane was looking at a picture that hung on the wall.

"Come and look at these trees," she said. "They reach to the top of the picture."

John said, "The trees are so tall that we can see only their trunks and some low branches. But small ones would not look well in the space the artist used."

"What is the woman doing?" asked Jane.

"She is taking care of the sheep," said Polly.

Then John pointed out how well the different things in the picture were arranged.

"Look," he said. "The sheep fill a large space on the right side of the picture. The green grass fills a space on the left side."

"This shows us one way to plan a picture," said Polly. "Now I will help Jane."

Polly took a piece of paper and showed Jane how to draw a landscape with a house and trees.

"Oh, I can do that now!" cried Jane.

Here is the picture Polly helped Jane make. Why is it better than Jane's picture on page 59?

A Landscape without Color

Here is a landscape which does not have colors. But it is a lovely picture. Notice how beautifully its light and dark spaces are arranged.

Different kinds of gray are used in these spaces. The tree and the grass in the foreground are very dark gray. They are almost black.

The row of trees farther back and the bridge in the background are dark gray and middle gray. The sky is a lighter gray, and the water is still lighter.

The tree trunks in this picture have lines that go up and down. Lines that go up and down are called vertical lines.

Find some vertical lines in the water.

Notice the place where the sky seems to meet the ground. This is called the horizon. It makes a line that goes across the picture.

A line which goes across, like the horizon, is called a horizontal line.

There are horizontal lines in the water. Find them.

Pictures often have both horizontal and vertical lines. These two kinds of lines look very well together.

It is best not to have all the horizontal lines in the same part of a picture. They should be arranged so that they look well with the vertical lines in the picture.

The horizontal and vertical lines in this landscape are well arranged. They help to make the picture look interesting.

An Artist Who Was a Teacher

Artists paint, draw, or model beautiful things. Some artists are also teachers. They teach other people how to paint, draw, or model.

Walter Sargent was an artist and a teacher of art. He painted landscapes that were shown at many different art exhibits. He showed other people how to draw and paint, too.

Mr. Sargent helped many people to see the beauty of the out-of-doors. He showed them how to sketch and paint some of the lovely things they saw.

Mr. Sargent was always looking for beautiful things in the out-of-doors. When he saw a tree that he liked, he noticed its shape, its trunk, and its leaves. He looked at its shadows. Then he made a drawing which helped him remember how the tree looked.

Before Mr. Sargent began to paint a picture, he made a sketch which showed the things he wanted to put into it. A sketch helps an artist plan a picture before he paints it.

On the next page is a pencil drawing that Mr. Sargent made. It is not a finished picture. It is a sketch.

Walter Sargent.

This sketch was made at noon. It shows the way the sunshine and shadows looked to Mr. Sargent at that hour of the day.

Notice that Mr. Sargent drew the trees large enough so that they look well in the space.

Here is a painting that Mr. Sargent made. The name of this landscape is "A Pool in the Woods."

The lovely colors in this painting make it very beautiful. Notice the cool colors of the sky.

The trees in the sunshine have red-orange and yellow-orange leaves.

Some of the trees in the foreground are in the shadow. We see violet and red-violet in them. The colors in shadow are darker than those we see in the sunshine.

The pool of water in the foreground is like a mirror that shows the colors of the sky and the trees.

This picture has some beautiful in-between colors.

What colors are in the background?

Name some other colors you see in the picture.

Mr. Sargent arranged the light and the dark spaces in this picture very beautifully. Where do you see light spaces?

Where do you see dark spaces?

The shapes of the trees are interesting, also. Notice the lines made by the trunks and branches. The trees fit well in the space that Mr. Sargent used.

This painting shows the beauty of the out-of-doors as an artist saw it.

Walter Sargent.

67

Landscapes

If I could paint as artists do,
   I'd paint a sunny sky of blue;
I'd paint some clouds with pink and gold
   To tint the edge of every fold;
I'd paint some flowers, trees, and grass,
   Blown by the dancing winds that pass,
And mirror pools all blue and brown,
   That turn my landscapes upside down.

Artists and Their Landscapes

This part of your art book has told you how artists draw and paint outdoor scenes. What is a picture of an outdoor scene called?

On one page you saw a famous picture of an outdoor scene. Do you remember the name of the man who painted it? If not, look at page 54.

Some of the pictures in this part of your art book have beautiful colors. But on page 62 you saw a landscape in black, white, and gray.

You have learned that artists make their pictures beautiful by arranging the light and the dark spaces in them.

Look again at the picture on page 62. How well the light and the dark spaces are arranged! What other things do you admire in it?

Look at the picture of the woman and her sheep on page 60. Where do you see vertical lines in this painting?

Where do you see horizontal lines?

Find an artist's sketch in this part of your book.

An artist's painting is different from a camera picture. Tell one way in which it is different.

Look at the landscape by Sargent on page 67. Give three reasons why this is a beautiful picture.

69

Part Four ARCHITECTURE

HERBERT
RUDEEN

The Boys' Club House

Next to Billy Cook's house there was a large lot that Billy and his friends used as a playground. In one corner of the lot they had put up a small building, which they called their club house.

One Saturday evening the boys were all playing games near the club house. Billy's father came over to them.

He smiled and said, "Boys, you will soon have to move your things out of the club house. In a few days the workmen are coming to start a new building on this lot."

The boys all felt very unhappy.

"Oh, Father!" cried Billy. "We have good times in our club house. Must we give it up?"

"I'm afraid you must," said his father. "But wait until you hear what is going to be built instead. Then you will be glad to give up your club house."

The boys looked at Billy's father and saw his smiling face.

"Tell us what is going to be built!" cried Jack in an excited voice.

"Please do, Mr. Cook!" said Jim.

"Let's go inside, boys," said Mr. Cook. "I'll tell you all about it."

So Billy's father and the boys went into the club house to have a talk.

"A new church will soon be built on this lot," said Mr. Cook.

"It is a big lot," said Billy. "Couldn't we keep just one little corner of it for our club house?"

Mr. Cook answered, "No, I'm afraid not. This church will be a fine, large building. It would not look at all well on a small lot.

"All of this space will be needed to make the building look well. There will be a lawn and trees and bushes around the new church."

Billy laughed as he thought how queer their little old club house would look standing beside a beautiful big church.

"Do you suppose we could build a new club house in some other place?" he asked. "All the boys feel sorry to give up their old club house."

Mr. Cook was still smiling.

"I have a surprise for you," he said. "Next to the new church there will be another building."

He opened a roll of blue paper that he had been carrying. "Here are the architect's plans," he said. "Look at them and see if you can tell what the surprise is."

The boys looked at the plans.

"Oh!" cried Jack. "The other building is a club house. Look! On the plan it says 'Boys' Club Room,' and in another place it says 'Girls' Club Room.' Isn't that a fine surprise!"

"Yes," answered Mr. Cook. "When the new buildings are finished, we shall have a beautiful church and a fine club house.

"You boys will have a much better place for your good times than you have now.

"The new club house will be built of stone. It will be a fine building, and the people of this town will be proud of it."

All the boys were excited.

"What fun we shall have in the new club room!" they cried.

Shapes That Architects Use

Architects use many shapes in planning buildings.

Look at the three small drawings on this page. Such shapes are called rectangles. A rectangle has four sides. But not all rectangles are alike.

This one is called a horizontal rectangle because its longer lines are horizontal.

Windows and doors usually have the shape of rectangles. Most of them are vertical rectangles. They are like the drawing you see at the right. Why do you think this is called a vertical rectangle?

Rectangles that have four sides alike are called squares. Here is a drawing that shows a square. Its four sides are alike.

Look at some different buildings to see if you can find walls that are horizontal rectangles, vertical rectangles, or squares.

This shape is called a triangle. It has three sides. If you will look at different buildings, you will see how architects use triangles.

Windows usually are rectangles. But sometimes a window has the shape of a circle, like this.

The top of a window may be shaped like a half circle. Then we say it is an arched window. A door may be arched, too.

Below are some architects' sketches of different parts of a building. Name some shapes that are used.

Buildings

Buildings in the city
Stretch themselves so high
They seem almost to bump their heads
Up against the sky.

Buildings in the country,
Just the other way,
Seem cuddled down behind the hills,
To hide themselves away.

Town and Country Buildings

Dick and Sally live in the country. This farmhouse is their home.

It is a large, light yellow house with a porch in front. Notice the tall white pillars that hold up the roof of the porch.

There are windows in the roof. What shape are they?

What other shapes can you find as you look at the building?

This house has a lawn with large trees on it, and there are flowers near the porch and along the fence.

This picture shows some of the other buildings on the farm.

The large building is a barn. You can see many different shapes in it.

The left end of the barn looks like a square with a triangle above it. The door is a vertical rectangle.

Near the barn is a tall building with curved walls. The floor inside is a circle, and Sally says that the roof makes her think of an ice-cream cone upside down.

Dick and Sally live near the little town of Glen Falls. Sometimes they go to town with their mother and father.

In Glen Falls the stores, the bank, and the office buildings are all on one street.

The stores are low. They look like a row of rectangles along the sidewalk. Some of these buildings have flat roofs.

The bank in Glen Falls is light-colored and has two pillars in front.

Find some different shapes in these buildings.

Franklin Booth.

This picture shows a street with small houses like those in Glen Falls.

What shapes do you see in these buildings?

Notice the large trees that grow along the streets of this town.

A Picture of a Church

A well-known artist painted this beautiful picture.

The painting shows a church with trees around it. The white building and the autumn trees are bright in the sunshine.

In this building you can find many of the interesting shapes that architects use. The front wall is a square, and above it we see a triangle.

What shape is the window in this triangle?

What kinds of windows do you see in the tower of the church?

What is the shape of each doorway?

Where do you see horizontal lines and vertical lines in this building?

At the front of the building are four pillars, which help make it beautiful.

This church is made of wood. Churches are often built of brick or stone, too.

Look at churches and other buildings near your home. Are they made of brick or stone or wood?

Name some of the shapes that the architects used in these buildings.

Childe Hassam.

83

Buildings in the City

Barbara March's home is in a large city. She lives with her father and mother in the house on top of this building. Many other people also have their homes in this tall brick building.

Most people who live in big buildings in the city do not have gardens. But Barbara has a garden! It is on the flat roof around her home.

Barbara's father had grass, small trees, and flowers put on the roof. That made a roof garden. There are window gardens on the building, too.

Barbara often goes to the playground or to the park. Many of her friends go there also. They have good times together.

Sometimes Barbara visits friends who live in another part of the city. They have houses with lawns and trees around them.

These houses are not so close together as the buildings in the part of the city where Barbara lives. They are more like the ones we see in smaller cities or towns.

There are many kinds of tall buildings in a large city. Barbara often visits her father's office. It is in a building that is even taller than the one you see in this picture.

Courtesy "Fashions of the Hour."   Pierre Brissaud.

On the next page is a picture which Barbara often looks at. It hangs in her father's office.

The picture shows another part of the city in which she lives. There are two kinds of buildings in it. Those in the foreground are old. They are made of bricks and are built close together.

These old buildings look like many rectangles side by side.

Behind these buildings are some that are much higher. They are new office buildings. One of them has a tower. This building is so tall that the top of the tower does not even show in the picture.

Most of the buildings shown in this picture are made of brick or stone. In all these buildings there are rows of windows. What shape are they?

There are no big yards around the buildings in this part of the city. But the picture shows a small park with a fence around it. It has many trees.

People who live in the city enjoy their parks very much. The parks make open spaces between the buildings.

This picture was painted by an artist who liked the straight lines, the shapes, and the colors she saw as she looked at these city buildings. She made a beautiful picture.

Courtesy John Herron Art Institute, Indianapolis, Indiana.   Felicie Howell.

87

One day while Barbara was in her father's office, an architect came to see Mr. March.

Mr. March was busy, and so the architect talked to Barbara for a little while. She showed him the picture on the wall.

The architect said, "The buildings in this picture show many of the shapes that architects use. Some of them look almost as if they had been made of blocks."

Then the man made a line drawing for the little girl.

The drawing that the architect made is shown on the next page. It shows the vertical and horizontal lines in the painting. This drawing shows the rectangles, squares, and triangles that the artist saw when she planned the picture.

Barbara enjoyed naming the different shapes in the drawing. Can you name them?

Look at some pictures of buildings. Try to find the different shapes you have been reading about.

Look at your home, your school, your church, and a bank. Tell about some of the shapes you see in them.

89

Making a House Look Beautiful

You have learned about some of the different things that make a house look beautiful.

First of all, the architect must plan the shapes of the different parts of the house so that they will look well together.

Picture 1 on page 91 shows a house that looks almost like a box.

Picture 2 shows how an architect made this house look better. He built more rooms and put in more windows. He used different shapes, and he arranged these shapes so that they would look well together.

Picture 3 shows how colors can make a house look better. The walls are yellow-orange. The roof is brown, and the shutters are green. These colors look well together.

Picture 4 shows the house with a green lawn, a neat walk, and beautiful trees, bushes, and flowers. All these things help make a house look well.

At first the little house was not very pretty. In the last picture it looks lovely.

Find some pictures of buildings in this book. Tell why you like one of these buildings.

Ernest D. Roth.

Things You Have Learned about Buildings

You have learned the names of some shapes that are used in buildings. Name as many of these shapes as you can.

Look at page 75 and page 76 to see if you have forgotten any.

Now look at the picture on page 92.

In the background of this picture is a famous old church. It is built on a hill, and its lovely lines can be seen against the sky.

This church is beautiful because its different parts look well together.

In the foreground of this picture there are other buildings. Look at these buildings. What shapes do you see in them?

Find some arches in the bridge.

You have learned three ways in which buildings can be made beautiful. This picture shows buildings with lovely lines and shapes.

Find a picture that shows buildings with pretty colors.

Find one that shows buildings with trees and lawns around them.

HERBERT
RUDEEN

Part Five · D E S I G N

Bob and Walter in the City

One summer Bob and Walter went on a trip with their father and mother. As they started out in the car, Father said, "I shall go slowly, so that we can enjoy the many beautiful things that we see along the way."

First they went through the country. They could see fields and trees of many different kinds of green. Sometimes there were rows of trees along the road.

The buildings in the country were not very tall. Often there were lovely trees and yards around the houses.

After a while they came to a large city.

"This street is not half so pretty as the country roads," said Walter. "In the country there are big trees along the roads. But there are no trees on this street."

"Some city streets have trees," said Father. "After a while we shall see some of them."

"I should like to see the stores," said Mother.

So Father drove the car down a busy street where there were many cars and many people. The buildings on both sides of the street were very tall.

"May we go into one of the stores?" asked Bob.

"Yes," said Mother. "These big stores are full of beautiful things which were designed by artists. I want you to see some of them."

Mother took the boys to one of the stores.

When they came back to the car, Walter said, "We saw some wonderful toys. Bob and I got an engine. Mother bought a bag, and we have a package for you, too."

Father said, "In a city you will see many
different things that were designed by artists. We
are going to look at some lovely streets and
buildings that artists have planned."

They drove on, and soon came to a wide street.
There were trees, grass, and flowers in the middle
and along each side of it.

"How beautiful this street is!" said Mother.
"Everything has been arranged so that it looks well.
The people who live here must enjoy this street."

Father drove on down the street until they came to a tall building that was decorated with designs over the doors and windows. Here he stopped the car.

"What a fine building!" said Walter. "Are we going to get out and look at it?"

"Yes," replied Father. "We are going to stay here over night. You boys may go inside with your mother and wait while I find a place to park the car."

When Walter and Bob went into the beautiful building, they saw a large room.

"Look," said Mother. "This room is beautifully decorated. The floor has an all-over design of squares. The rugs have lovely colors and designs, and the walls are decorated, too."

"Oh, see the design around the top of the room!" cried Walter.

"And there are some doors that have designs, too," said Bob.

When their father came into the room, the boys pointed out the different designs they had noticed.

"Buildings like this are often decorated on the inside and on the outside," said Father. "It is another way that artists have of making a city beautiful."

This is a picture of the room where Bob and Walter waited for their father.

Where do you see some all-over designs in the room?

Find a border design and tell where you found it.

Look for designs that decorate rooms in your home, your church, or your school. Try to find both border designs and all-over designs.

Look for designs on the outside of buildings, too. Tell about the designs you have seen on different buildings.

A Bus Ride in the Park

The next morning Father said, "Today I think I'll take you boys for a ride on the top of a bus. We can go to almost any part of the city on a bus. But one of the prettiest rides is through the park."

"Let's go through the park!" cried the boys.

So Bob and Walter and their father got on a large green bus. They went up some steps in the bus, so that they could sit on the top. From there they saw many fine buildings along the streets.

Soon they came to a large open place with lovely green lawns and trees.

"Now we've come to the park!" said Father.

The children saw roads that curved in and out through the green lawns.

"How lovely the flower beds are!" said Walter. "There are flowers of many colors."

"Why, look!" cried Bob. "The flower beds make a design!"

On the next page is a picture that shows some flower beds which the boys saw from the bus.

Flower beds are planned by landscape artists to make the parks beautiful.

Notice, too, how the trees in the park are arranged. They make a beautiful background for the lawns, flowers, and paths.

In one place there is a statue in front of the trees.

When you go to a park, try to help keep it beautiful. Do not leave anything on the lawns.

People come to a park to enjoy the beauty which has been planned for them. The lovely trees, flowers, statues, and buildings are for everyone to enjoy.

An Art Museum

This picture shows an art museum which is in one of our large cities.

It is a fine building of white stone.

The architects planned the building very well. Notice its form. It is low, and the front has the shape of a rectangle.

It has interesting lines, also. Above, you can see the lines of the roof. Some of these are horizontal. But there are two which do not go across like horizontal lines. They do not go straight up and down like vertical lines. We call them slanting lines.

This building is beautiful because it has lines that look well together. The slanting lines of the roof look well with the horizontal lines and the vertical lines of the building.

There are three horizontal lines across the top of the building just under the roof. The windows and the door are vertical rectangles, which look well with these lines.

All these lines help make the museum a beautiful building.

The building has only a little decoration, and that is placed where it looks best.

Over the windows there are designs which decorate the plain wall space. There are all-over designs in the openings under the windows.

But the most interesting part of all is the door. It is in the middle of the front wall. Around it there is a frame, which makes it look more important than the windows.

There is another design over the top of the door, and at each corner of the building there is a decoration made by a sculptor.

This building is just right for an art museum. It is as lovely as the things inside it.

Designs in an Art Museum

In an art museum there are pictures and statues and many other things for people to admire.

Some of the things in a museum have pretty designs. You may find pottery, baskets, rugs, cloth, and other things with designs.

For hundreds and hundreds of years people have put designs on cloth. Some designs on cloth are so beautiful or so interesting that people keep them for a great many years.

The next page shows a piece of cloth with a design that was made hundreds of years ago. The design has monkeys, fish, and birds. They are arranged in vertical rows.

Aren't the monkeys funny? They do not look like real monkeys. And the fish and the birds were not made to look like real fish and birds, but to give an interesting design. Notice that the monkeys, fish, and birds are shown over and over again.

This design is different from those we see in our homes today. But we often see cloth with designs arranged in rows.

On page 106 you will find a picture of some other things you might see in an art museum.

Courtesy Museum of Fine Arts, Boston, Massachusetts.

Courtesy Doulton & Co., Limited, Burslem, England.

The vases in this picture were made of clay. Vases and bowls of this kind are called pottery.

Notice their beautiful forms. Some of the pieces have curved lines, while others have lines that are nearly straight.

Pottery is made in many colors. In this picture you see pottery of different kinds of red.

Some of this pottery is plain, and some has decorations. An artist may decorate a piece of pottery with a design.

Many art museums have wonderful exhibits of pottery, such as vases and bowls. The forms, colors, and decorations of these pieces of pottery were planned by artists.

Courtesy Art Education Press, Inc., New York.

Some art museums have exhibits of baskets. The basket in this picture is in a museum.

We call it an Indian basket because it was planned and made by an Indian woman.

It is beautifully made and is decorated with designs. Around the middle there is a row of dark figures with a light background.

How is the design at the top of the basket different from the design at the bottom?

Beautiful Doors

Designs are often used to decorate the doors of buildings. On the next page you see some doors with an all-over design.

The doors are in a famous building in a far-away city. They were made a long time ago by a great artist. They are so beautiful that they have never been forgotten. Many people go to see them every year.

The doors are of heavy brown metal, and the design on them stands out from the background.

The design is arranged in rectangles, and around each rectangle there is a border. There is another border design on the frame of the doors.

Many buildings today have doors and windows decorated with designs. Sometimes you see windows that have designs of colored glass.

Different kinds of designs may be used for decoration. Some doors of wood have borders or all-over designs carved on them. And metal doors are often decorated with designs.

Where can you see windows with colored glass?
What other parts of buildings have you seen decorated with designs?

Andrea Pisano.

Raphael.

A Famous Picture

This picture is known and admired everywhere.
It was painted by a great artist named Raphael.

The first thing you see as you look at this picture is a Baby cuddled close in His Mother's arms. He is in the middle of the picture.

The colors of His clothes and of the Mother's sleeve are brighter than the other colors. The bright colors help make Him the most important part of the picture.

The older boy behind the Baby is in the background. There are shadows on his head and on his clothes.

There are many lovely colors in Raphael's picture. The colors in the Mother's face are like those we see in the Baby's face, arm, and legs. These colors are very beautiful against the dark background.

How well Raphael planned his picture! He painted it in a circle, and he used lines and spaces that look well in a round picture.

See how the Mother's head is bending over the Baby, as she cuddles Him in her arms. Her arm makes a curve. The Baby's arm fits into this curve.

Raphael used many curved lines because they look better than straight lines in a round picture.

Notice how all of the curved lines have been arranged to go well together.

On this page is a drawing which shows the curved lines of Raphael's painting.

Look again at the colored picture. Find the curved lines in it.

The children cut the letters they needed out of colored paper. Then they arranged them nicely on their book covers.

Billy liked Marie's flower design. He said, "My book cover is going to have a design on it, too." Then he made a design of triangles.

George made a different design for his cover.

Miss Hood said, "I like these covers because the letters are not too small or too large to look well in the spaces. The designs are pretty, too."

Find Marie's book cover in the picture above. Why do you like it?

Do you like George's or Billy's cover better? Tell why you like it.

Posters and Lettering

Here are some pictures that show how lettering can be arranged in pleasing ways.

These pictures are called posters. Notice the poster at the left. The words fill the space at the top and the bottom. The letters at the top are not so big as those at the bottom.

In the middle poster the more important words are in larger letters.

The poster at the right has white lettering which decorates the dark space at the bottom.

Both straight and curved lines were used in making these posters. All of them are interesting because the lines and spaces are well arranged. Good lettering helps make them look well.

Designs Are All around You

Designs are used to decorate many things. Try to find some designs in your home.

When you get up in the morning, you may see designs on the wall paper of your bedroom.

When you put on your clothes, you may find that there is a design on your dress or on your sweater.

At the table you may see designs on the dishes and on the tablecloth.

What designs do you see in the picture above?

Part Six
ART IN SCHOOL AND HOME

The New Schoolroom

Miss Hubbard and the children in her class had just moved into a new room, but they were unhappy.

"Oh, Miss Hubbard!" cried Patty. "I wish we could have stayed in our pretty room."

Billy said, "This room is not half so nice as our old one. It is clean, but it isn't pretty."

"I think you will enjoy your new room when you know what we are going to do," said Miss Hubbard. "Wouldn't you like to plan a way to make it look better?"

"Oh, yes!" cried all the children.

"May we plan just what we like?" asked Nancy.

"Yes," said Miss Hubbard. "You may decide what you would like to do to the room.

119

"I think we can make it look even better than the one we've had."

Frank said, "Then I'm glad we moved. It will be fun to see how pretty we can make this room."

"What shall we do first?" asked Jane.

"First, you should plan the color of the walls," said the teacher. "They are the background of the room. When you have decided on the color of the walls, you can plan the other things to look well with them."

"May we paint the walls?" asked Jane.

"You may plan how you want to have them painted," Miss Hubbard replied. "While we are having our vacation, some men will come and do the painting."

Miss Hubbard showed the children a chart from which they could choose the colors they wanted.

"Most of the colors on this chart are tints," she said. "Walls and ceilings are usually painted in tints."

The children looked carefully at the chart and talked about the different colors.

At last they chose a green tint for the walls.

"What do you want for the ceiling?" asked Miss Hubbard. "The colors near the top of the room are usually lighter than those near the floor."

The children chose a lighter green tint for the ceiling.

"Don't you think green woodwork and a gray floor would look well with our walls and ceiling?" asked Miss Hubbard.

"Oh, yes!" cried the children. Then they all looked around to see what else they wanted.

Suddenly Betty said, "Some of these desks are green, some are brown, and five of them are yellow. Wouldn't the room look better if all the desks were the same color?"

"Indeed it would," said Miss Hubbard. "Pieces of furniture of the same kind usually match in color.

"We must decide which desks look best in the room. The desks that are not the right color can be changed."

The children decided to have green desks in the room, because they would look well with the walls, woodwork, and floor.

"We need a place to keep our books," said Jane. "Do you suppose we could have some book shelves at the side of the room?"

The children thought this was a good plan. They wanted some window boxes, too.

"We can have bright flowers in the window boxes," said Sally. "Flowers help to decorate a room."

"You have planned the room very well indeed," Miss Hubbard told the children. "When you come back from your spring vacation, this room will look different."

While the children were enjoying their vacation, some men built book shelves and window boxes and painted the schoolroom.

When the children came back, they were happy to see the room.

"Doesn't our room look much better than it did before?" said John.

"Yes," replied Miss Hubbard. "But we still need some things to make it beautiful. Wouldn't you like to choose some curtains?"

The children chose rose-colored curtains. They thought the room needed some warm colors with the cool green of the walls and woodwork.

When they had hung the curtains, Mary said, "We still do not have enough warm colors. Couldn't we have some vases or bowls with warm colors?"

"Pictures sometimes have warm colors, too," said Ann. "Couldn't we have another picture?"

"You thought of the very same thing I did!" cried the teacher. "A large picture would look well in the plain wall space at the side of the room.

"I asked a man at the art store to let us look at some prints. Here they are."

The children looked at the different pictures.

At last George said, "These are all pretty. How shall we choose one?"

Miss Hubbard said, "Look at the space where you wish to hang the picture. A picture that is the same or nearly the same shape will look best in the space."

Courtesy Art Education Press, Inc., New York.

Jean Francois Millet.

"Shouldn't we think of the colors in our room, too?" asked Helen.

"Yes," said Miss Hubbard. "Our picture should look well with the colors we have."

The children chose a picture called "The First Steps." It was made by a great artist named Millet, who liked to draw and paint scenes in the country.

The picture shows a baby that is just learning to walk. The father and mother are helping the baby.

The children liked the figures in this picture.

Miss Hubbard said, "Millet often put figures in his paintings.

"Millet used many warm colors in this picture. The mother and father both have rose color in their clothes. In the foreground we see warm brown, and there are tints of warm colors in the background."

The colors in this picture looked well with the colors of the schoolroom. It was the right shape for the space on the wall, too.

"You have chosen a lovely picture," said Miss Hubbard. "Now let us hang it."

They hung the picture just high enough so that the children could all see it well.

As they finished with the work, a man opened the door and carried in a large box. On it there was a card which said, "For the children of Miss Hubbard's room."

"Oh, oh, what is in it? May we open the box, Miss Hubbard?" cried the excited children.

When the box was opened, the teacher and the children saw a beautiful statue. There was a tall stand for it, too.

"Oh, isn't this statue lovely!" cried Betty. "Someone knew just what we needed."

Tom saw his teacher smiling.

"Miss Hubbard knows where it came from!" he cried.

Miss Hubbard laughed. "I shall have to tell you," she said. "The Mothers' Club sent the statue because they wanted to help make this a beautiful room."

The children admired their new statue very much.

John carried the stand to the front of the room. "Let's put it here," he said. "We want it where we can all see it."

Ann laughed. "But we don't want it where we'll all fall over it," she said. "People need plenty of space to walk across the front of the room."

"Ann is right," said Miss Hubbard. "Nothing looks well when it is in the way."

So the children decided to put the statue in one of the front corners of the room. That was just the place for it.

Miss Hubbard and the children felt very proud of the room they had made beautiful.

"Everything looks just right, doesn't it?" said John.

Patty said, "This room makes me feel like working."

126

Miss Hubbard smiled and said, "We are always happiest when things about us are beautiful. You like this room because it has colors that look well together.

"The woodwork, the floor, and the walls look pretty together. The furniture is well arranged. There are lovely pictures, books, a statue, and some flowers."

The children were as happy as they could be in their beautiful schoolroom.

"I like this much better than our old room," said Robert. "That room was pretty, but we made this one pretty ourselves."

The Beauty Corner

Have you ever seen a beauty corner in a schoolroom? The children of Miss Hubbard's room had one.

In their room the children had a table. On it they put beautiful things which they enjoyed looking at. Only a few things were put there at one time.

Sometimes there was a picture on a small easel. Sometimes there was a vase or a bowl.

One day Ann brought a table cover.

"Mother said we might have this in our beauty corner for a day," she told Miss Hubbard. "It is a cover that my aunt brought back from a country far away."

"What pretty colors and designs it has!" cried Betty.

Bobby's mother gave him some book-ends for his birthday. Each one was an elephant carved out of heavy stone. The book-ends were so pretty that Bobby put them in the beauty corner.

Ruth brought some flowers. "Flowers help make a room look well," she said. "I will put these in our beauty corner."

The children were always finding lovely things to bring to the beauty corner. Pottery, books, metal vases, Indian baskets, and small rugs were among the pretty things they brought.

Nearly every day the children of Miss Hubbard's room found something new to enjoy in the beauty corner.

Name something you could put in a beauty corner in your schoolroom.

Setting the Table

It was a rainy Sunday afternoon in September.

"Oh, dear!" said Jim, putting down his book. "It is still raining. I don't feel like reading any more. Can't you think of something else to do?"

Barbara looked up from her magazine. "Here are some pictures of supper tables," she said. "See, Jim! Aren't they lovely?"

"Yes," replied Jim, as he looked at the pictures. "They are pretty."

Barbara jumped up. "I know," she said. "It is almost supper time. Father and Mother will soon come home. Let's surprise them. We can set the table before they get here. Let's make our table as pretty as the ones in the magazine."

"That will be fun!" cried Jim. "Come on." The children ran quickly to the dining-room.

"Let's use the doilies and napkins with the blue borders," said Barbara.

She put a doily at each place, and beside each doily she put a folded napkin.

Jim went to the cupboard and looked at his mother's dishes.

"Which dishes will look best with these doilies?" he asked.

"Here are some dishes with light yellow edges," said Barbara. "Yellow and blue look very well together."

Jim put a plate and some silver at each place.

When Barbara saw what Jim had done, she said, "Oh, Jim! You have put some of the plates on the left side of the doily and some on the right. That doesn't look well.

"All the places at the table should look just alike. Every plate should be in the middle of the doily, and the silver should be arranged the same way at every place."

"I see," said Jim. "Setting a table is just like making a design. You arrange the same things in the same way over and over again."

Then Jim placed the silver, the plates, and the glasses as he saw them in the magazine picture. He made all the places alike.

While Jim was doing this, Barbara arranged some yellow flowers in a bowl. She put them in the middle of the table.

As the two children were admiring the supper table, they heard steps on the sidewalk.

"That must be Father and Mother," cried Jim. "Quick! Let's hide behind the curtains."

Then Mother opened the dining-room door, and they heard her say, "Oh, my! What a pretty supper table! Who could have set it?"

Jim and Barbara ran out from behind the curtains.

"We did!" they cried.

"It was fun," said Barbara. "May we set the table for supper every Sunday?"

"Yes, indeed," replied Mother. "I think all of us would enjoy eating our Sunday supper at a table as beautiful as this."

The pictures on this page show two different ways in which supper tables can be arranged. Tell what has been done to make each table look well.

A Picture of Flowers

Magazine covers often have pictures of flowers. On the next page is a picture that an artist painted for a magazine cover.

It shows some flowers in a glass vase. They have lovely colors and shapes.

Flowers which are carefully arranged look much better than flowers that are just put into a vase.

Notice how well the flowers in this picture are arranged.

Some of them are higher than others. Each flower and leaf looks as if it had plenty of room. The green leaves and stems are lovely with the bright colors of the flowers. Notice how the stems show through the glass.

The plain vase is a cool blue color. But you can hardly see the vase because of the way the flowers and leaves bend over its edge.

This picture has many in-between colors. What in-between colors do you see in it?

Sometimes pictures of flowers are framed and used to decorate our walls.

Look for flower pictures. When you find one, notice how the flowers in it are arranged.

Elizabeth Lansdell Hammell.

135

Arranging Flowers

Flowers help make a room look pretty. But they must be well arranged. Flowers with long stems should be put in a tall vase. Those with short stems should be in a low bowl.

The leaves and stems are often beautiful, too. When flowers are put in a vase or a bowl, some of the leaves and stems should show.

There should not be too many flowers in a vase. Each one should have plenty of room, so that it will look well.

Tell why the flowers in the picture above are well arranged.

Beauty at School and at Home

At home and at school we want lovely things to look at.

We try to choose pieces of furniture that go well together, and to arrange them so that they make a room look nice.

The things in a room should be carefully placed. Perhaps you can help your mother or your teacher arrange a room in your home or your school.

The colors in the room should go well together. Usually a room looks better if it has both warm and cool colors.

Tints and shades of the same color may often be used together.

We may choose beautiful pictures to hang on our walls. Statues, rugs, pottery, flowers, and curtains with lovely designs are among the other things which decorate our rooms.

At work or at play we enjoy having things in their places. A neat room always looks better than one that is not neat.

Read again the story "The New Schoolroom" and tell what the children did to make the room look better.

· *Part Seven* · COSTUME ·

The Three Princesses

Once upon a time there was a king who had three daughters. The princesses had many fine dresses. Some of these were even decorated with gold and silver, but the girls did not look beautiful.

This made the king feel very unhappy. At last he said, "If anyone can make my daughters look beautiful, I will give him a bag of gold."

In a short time a man came to the king.

He said, "Oh, king, I bring dew from a field of magic flowers. If your daughters will wash their faces in this dew, they will become beautiful."

Smiling, the king said, "If they are made beautiful by the dew, you shall have the gold."

But the dew from the magic flowers did not make the princesses look any different.

Next came a man with jewels, who said, "These will make your daughters look lovely."

The king smiled again and said, "If the jewels make the girls look beautiful, you shall have the gold."

But the jewels did not change the looks of the princesses.

At last a man said, "Oh, king, I know how to make your daughters look beautiful."

The king did not smile now. "I do not think anyone can make them look beautiful," he said. "But you may try if you wish."

The princesses were brought in. When the man looked at them, he started to laugh.

"Do not laugh at the princesses!" cried the king in a great voice.

"I am not laughing at them," said the man. "I am laughing to think that I shall soon have the gold."

He looked at the first princess, who had dark hair and dark eyes. Then he held some folds of rose-colored cloth over her dress. Suddenly she looked beautiful, and the king smiled again.

Then the man turned to the next princess. She had blue eyes and golden hair.

He held a piece of light blue cloth over her dress. Its color matched her eyes. In this color she looked beautiful, and the king's smile grew even brighter.

The last princess had red-brown hair and brown eyes. The man held up some folds of cloth of a light golden color.

"The cloth makes my daughters look beautiful!" cried the king. "It must be magic cloth."

"No, it is not magic cloth," the man replied. "There is no magic in what I do. You have seen each of your daughters with a color that is becoming to her.

"Your daughters have always been handsome. But no one could see their beauty, because they did not have the right kind of clothes."

"Then you must make some new clothes for the princesses," said the king.

"When the new dresses are ready, I shall give a grand ball and invite all their friends. Then we shall see if the three princesses really look beautiful."

So the man went away. For five days he was busy making new clothes for the king's daughters.

At last the day of the ball came. The king
was happy when he saw his three daughters.

The princess with dark hair and dark eyes wore
a rose-colored dress.

The princess with golden hair had a light green
dress, and the princess with red-brown hair was
dressed in white and tints of gold.

How handsome they all looked! Everyone said,
"The princesses are the most beautiful girls here."

The next day the man came to get his gold.

The king said, "First, tell me your secret for making my daughters beautiful."

The man bowed and answered, "The princesses should wear colors that are becoming to them. The princess with dark hair and eyes should wear colors near the warm part of the rainbow. The right kind of green will make her look lovely, too.

"The princess with golden hair and blue eyes should wear light colors that are near the blue, green, and violet part of the rainbow.

"And the princess with red-brown hair should never wear red. She will look lovely in white, light yellow, light orange, or golden brown."

The king was so pleased that he thanked the man and gave him the bag of gold.

A Real Princess

A long time ago there was a real king who lived in a country far away. He had sons as well as daughters.

Among the king's friends was a great artist. He painted many pictures of the king and his family.

One of his pictures shows a son of the king on his pony. You can see this picture in Art Stories, Book Two.

The figure painting on the next page is a picture of one of the king's daughters.

It shows the kind of clothes that a princess wore three hundred years ago.

This dress is very different from children's clothes today. And still it looks beautiful on the little princess. The dress is made of gray silk. There is dark lace at the neck and on the sleeves.

The skirt is long and very wide. On it there is a lovely design in rose color. Don't the gray and rose look pretty together?

The rose color on the skirt matches the rosy cheeks of the little princess. The gray of the silk makes the rose color look bright. The dark lace matches the dark eyes of the princess.

Velasquez.

145

The Blue Boy

Here is a picture of a boy who lived almost two hundred years ago.

Do you wonder why this picture is admired after so many years? It is a beautiful painting, which was made by an artist named Gainsborough.

This picture is called "The Blue Boy." It is one of the most famous paintings Gainsborough ever made.

Notice the boy's handsome clothes. He has on a blue silk suit, which fits closely. The blue of his clothes looks well with his brown hair and eyes.

There is lace at the neck and on the sleeves of his suit. On his shoes there are large bows.

In Gainsborough's time many boys wore clothes like this.

Notice the large hat the boy is holding. Such hats are sometimes called Gainsborough hats because this great artist put them into many of his pictures.

A boy of today would feel queer wearing a Gainsborough hat. But long ago boys often wore these large hats when they were dressed in their best clothes.

Thomas Gainsborough.

147

The Costume Party

Jack and Ruth Means ran to their mother.

"Mother, Mother!" Ruth cried. "Saturday is Patty's birthday, and she has invited us both to a costume party. She wants all the girls and boys to come dressed like story-book people."

"Won't that be fun!" said Mrs. Means, smiling. "What story-book people do you want to be?"

"Well," said Jack, "we'll have to think a little. We both want to be people out of the same story, don't we, Ruth?"

"Oh, yes," answered Ruth.

"But I want to be somebody funny. What funny story-book people are there?"

Then she began to laugh. "I know!" she cried. "We can be Jack Spratt and his wife. 'Jack Spratt could eat no fat.' Why, that fits you, Jack! You don't like fat."

"But how will people know who we are?" asked Jack.

"Oh, we can carry a platter," said Ruth, "a clean platter! Now, how shall we dress?"

"Jack Spratt didn't eat fat. So he must have been thin," said Mrs. Means. "For this reason Jack's costume should make him look tall and thin. It will do so if it has lines that go up and down."

"If I am Mrs. Spratt, I should look fat," said Ruth. "What will make me look fat?"

"A large design," replied Mrs. Means. "Large designs make people look bigger than they really are. A very wide skirt will make you look fatter, too."

Ruth jumped up and cried, "Oh, I can hardly wait! May we make our costumes today?"

"I think so," answered her mother. "We will go right down town for the things we need."

When they got home, Mrs. Means helped the children make their costumes of colored paper.

149

Jack's costume had light and dark stripes which ran up and down. He had a tall hat with stripes to match.

When he tried on his costume, Ruth cried, "My, you look tall and thin, Mr. Spratt!"

Ruth's costume was light green with large white flowers. It had a very wide skirt.

Her mother helped her make a white cap, with a green bow on each side. The bows made her face look round and fat. Jack thought she looked just like Mrs. Spratt.

When Saturday came, Ruth and Jack put on their costumes and took their mother's large platter. They had to laugh when they looked at each other.

At Patty's house they saw many other children.

Patty looked very tall and thin in a pink and white striped dress. At first Ruth didn't know who she was supposed to be. Then she saw that Patty had a toy lamb.

Ruth said, "Patty has a lamb. Maybe she's Mary who had a little lamb."

Dick and Ann came as the king of hearts and the queen of hearts. They had white costumes with a design of big red hearts.

Ruth thought, "Now I see why Mother said that a big design makes anyone look larger. The big hearts make Ann and Dick look fat."

Old Mother Hubbard's dress had large circles on it. The wide skirt made her look fat, too.

When Ray came in, he was bending over a crooked stick. His suit was striped, but the stripes didn't go up and down. They slanted this way and that way.

Jack said, "I think Ray is the crooked man, because the stripes make him look crooked."

After they had eaten their ice cream and cake, Patty's mother said, "All the costumes are so good that it is hard to choose the best. But many of the children like Jack Spratt and his wife best.

"I think their costumes must be best because Jack looks so thin, his wife looks so fat, and their platter is so clean."

Choosing Your Clothes

Choosing the clothes we wear is important.

Try to wear colors that look well on you. What colors do you think you can wear best?

Why do you think these colors look well on you?

You should not wear too many different colors at the same time. A girl who wears a brown hat, a blue dress, a green coat, and red shoes has on too many colors.

The colors of the different things you wear should look well together. Some of the things you wear should match in color.

You may wear tints and shades of the same color, or you may choose warm and cool colors that look well together. Name some colors that you might wear together.

Small designs usually look better on boys and girls than large designs. Can you tell why?

Always keep your clothes clean and neat, so that they will look well.

Try to wear the right kind of clothes for the different things you do.

Party clothes are not the right kind to wear to school. Play suits would not do for church or school.

Party Clothes and School Clothes

Look at the children in the picture on the next page. One of the boys is dressed for a party. Can you tell which boy it is?

One girl has a beautiful yellow dress. She does not wear this dress to school because it is her best dress. It is too fine to wear every day.

The other girl has on a pretty dress that can be washed. It is a good dress for school.

John is not shown in the picture. He has a brown suit and a blue sweater. He wants a new cap. "Shall I buy a green one or a brown one?" he asks. Which color should he choose? Why?

Sally has a beautiful pink silk dress with lace on the sleeves. "Shall I wear my coat or my sweater with this dress?" she asks. Which should she choose? Give one reason for your answer.

Billy has white shoes, black shoes, and high brown shoes. He is wearing a white suit. Which shoes would look best with his suit?

Marie has a dark blue dress with red on it. She has a light yellow dress, too. One day Grandmother gave her a yellow hair ribbon. With which dress should she wear the ribbon? Why?

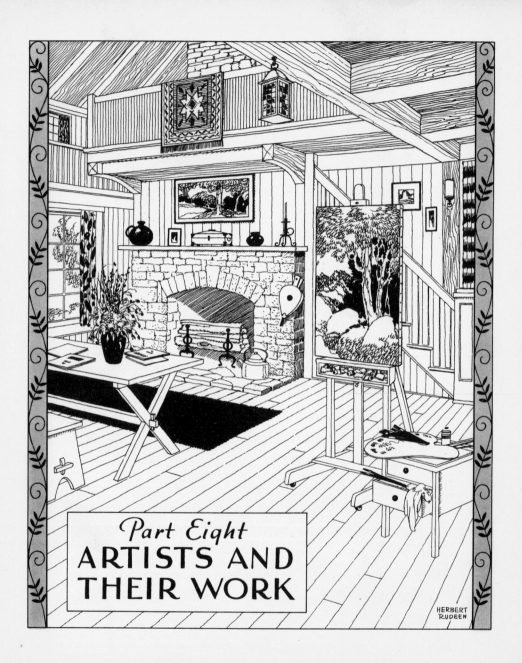

Part Eight
ARTISTS AND
THEIR WORK

HERBERT
RUDEEN

The Children's Art Program

One Friday afternoon many fathers and mothers went to the Frost School. They had been invited to come and see a surprise.

When they got to the school, they were taken into a big room where there was a stage. In front of the stage there were curtains.

All the fathers and mothers wondered what they were going to see.

At last Nancy came out in front of the curtains. She said, "Our program is called 'Art in Everyday Life.' It is going to show how things around us can be made beautiful.

"First, we are going to make some buildings."

All the mothers and fathers clapped their hands.

In a minute the curtains opened. At the back of the stage was a scene which the children had painted. It showed tall buildings against a blue sky.

Some of the children came on the stage carrying blocks of many shapes. Some blocks were large, and some were small. Some had sides shaped like squares, while others had sides shaped like rectangles. There were blocks with rounded tops, and blocks with ends shaped like triangles.

John stood at the front of the stage and said, "These blocks are like the forms which an architect uses when he designs a building.

"We are going to put the blocks together to make some buildings.

"When we've finished, you will see that buildings have interesting forms. You will see how these forms are used in designing buildings."

The children quickly put their blocks together at the front of the stage. Then they stepped back, and their parents saw a church, an office building, and a school. They were all built of blocks.

All the fathers and mothers clapped their hands.

The curtains closed, and when they opened again, the parents saw a plain room without any furniture.

Nancy came to the front of the stage and said, "This room does not look pretty now. But we are going to make it look pretty. First, we shall put some furniture, curtains, rugs, and pictures in it. Then we will arrange these things so that everything will look well."

Other children came on the stage, bringing things to put in the room. Some men carried in the large pieces of furniture.

In a few minutes the fathers and mothers saw a lovely room. It did not have too many things in it, and the pieces of furniture looked well together. They were well arranged, and the different colors were pretty together.

The parents all clapped their hands.

"I like that room! This program really does show beauty in the things around us!" one of the fathers said.

When the curtains closed again, Barbara stood in front of them.

She said, "We haven't time to show you all the ways in which we can make the things around us beautiful.

"But in the last part of our program you will see how clothes can be beautiful."

Then the curtains opened once more, and in came the children, dressed in clothes of different colors. What a parade it was! It made a wonderful end to the program.

After that everyone had ice cream and cake.

As the parents were leaving, they all talked about the program.

Mr. Jewel said, "I am glad we were invited to this program. It has really shown us how we can use art in everyday life."

161

A Picture of Flamingos

On the next page is a picture of birds. Birds like this are called flamingos. A flamingo has a beautiful color, and its shape is handsome, too.

The artist who made this picture likes to paint pictures of beautiful birds. He even goes to other countries to find different kinds of birds.

This artist has a garden where the birds can live happily while he paints pictures of them.

Flamingos are among the birds that he likes best, because they are so handsome and have such a lovely color.

These birds have long necks and long, crooked legs. The curved lines of their bodies are very beautiful.

In this picture the artist has shown three flamingos standing in water. The birds have been arranged so that they look well in the picture. They are made very large, so that they will fill the space.

Their color looks bright against the dark background. The water is like a mirror showing spots of the flamingos' color.

Courtesy of the artist.

Karl Plath.

163

How Books Are Made Beautiful

You have learned many things from your art book. You have read about artists and the many different kinds of work they do.

Have you ever known that artists help design books, too? They do many things to make books look lovely and interesting.

They design book covers. Notice the cover on your art book and the covers of other beautiful books.

When an artist designs a book cover, he chooses colors that look well together. Then he arranges the colors nicely.

He arranges the lettering beautifully, too. See how the letters in the title of your art book are arranged. The other lettering on the cover is placed so that it looks well with the title.

The inside cover pages of books are often decorated by artists. Find the all-over design that is on the inside cover pages of your art book.

The different things in this design have been arranged in squares. In many of these squares the artist put things that are found in the pictures of your book.

Name some of the different things you see on the inside cover pages.

Find the page at the beginning of this book which has the title of the book in large letters near the top. This is called the title page.

Often an artist decorates the title page with a border or another design. He arranges the lettering on the title page, too. Notice the title pages of books you read.

As you look through your art book, you will see many pictures. They are the work of artists, too.

There are prints of pictures by great artists like Corot, Gainsborough, Millet, and Raphael. Find these pictures in your art book and look at them again.

There are other pictures in Art Stories which were made by artists just for this book.

Some of these pictures have many colors. Look at the colored pictures on pages 16, 33, and 46.

There are other pictures that are black and white or black, white, and gray, like those on pages 26 and 48.

Find some pictures in the book that are line drawings. What pages are they on?

This book shows some camera pictures, too. The picture of the statue on page 45 and the one of the building on page 102 are camera pictures. These show you some work of architects and sculptors just as the camera sees it.

Lovely books are made for you to read, to look at, and to enjoy. Keep your books beautiful by taking good care of them.

James J. Shannon

VOCABULARY

The following list includes all the words used in *Art Stories, Book Three* that were not used in *Art Stories, Books One* and *Two*. Of these there are 198.

9
hide
among
behind
edge

10
easel
holds

11
five

12
hid
forgot

13
sweater

14
wheel

15
tints
shades
becomes
below

16
cottage
banks
wife

17
broke
we've

18
scene

19
trunks
soft
minute
shut

20
Frost
fairies
elf
stem

22
hour
glen
September's
Metcalf

24
Friday
class
quickly

25
chart
steps
instead

26
engine
point

27
also
well-known
such

29
pasture
fence
colt

30
thin
lead
sketching
short

31
I'd

33
Saturday
studio
full
posing

34
sailor
figure
body
finished

35
cook
cap
apron

36
pen
heavy
manes

38
flat
metal
itself

39
curl
neck

41
lettering

42
daughter
important
fills

44
Hood
wolf
carved
stone

46
million
steam
vessels
smoke

47
arranges

49
joke
landscapes
camera

52
left
means
decides

53
carefully

54
Corot

55
admired
forgotten

57
above
reason

58
teacher

59
unhappy

61
sheep

63
vertical
horizon
horizontal

64
Walter
Sargent

66
fit

68
fold
pass

71
club
lot
corner

72
felt
excited

73
lawn
suppose
feel

75
rectangle
square

76
triangle
circle
half
arched

77
stretch
bump
cuddled

78
Sally
porch
pillars

79
end
cream
cone

82
tower
brick

84
close

95
slowly
drove

96
wonderful
bag

98
decorated
replied
rugs

100
bus

102
museum

103
slanting
decoration
plain
frame

104
cloth
pottery
monkeys
fish

106
bowls

107
Indian
bottom

111
arms
sleeve
bending

113
Marie

114
title

116
posters
words

119
Hubbard

120
chose

121
desks

122
indeed

124
Millet

125
knock
set

126
plenty

130
Sunday
supper
doilies

131
plate
silver

134
hardly

139
princesses
dew
magic
jewels

141
handsome
invite

144
sons
silk
lace
skirt

146
Gainsborough

148
costume

149
Spratt
fat
platter

150
stripes

151
hearts
crooked

157
program
stage
life
clapped

158
parents

162
flamingos

INDEX OF ART CONTENT

(References are to pages)

---

*New in *Book Three*.   Subjects not starred were introduced in *Book One* or *Book Two*.

171